THE
Archive Photographs
SERIES

LEWISHAM

The Vicar's Hill Dairy at 1, The Pavement, Ladywell (now 218 Algernon Road), showing the proprietor James Haydon and his son Fred. Mr. Haydon was here from 1905 until the early 1930s. For The Pavement see page 95.

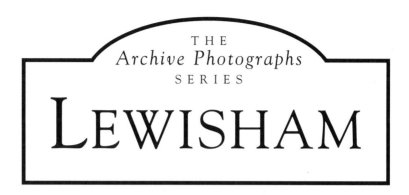

THE
Archive Photographs
SERIES

LEWISHAM

Compiled by
John Coulter and Barry Olley

CHALFORD

First published 1995
Copyright © John Coulter and Barry Olley, 1995

The Chalford Publishing Company
St Mary's Mill, Chalford,
Stroud, Gloucestershire, GL6 8NX

ISBN 0 7524 0059 2

Typesetting and origination by
The Chalford Publishing Company
Printed in Great Britain by
Redwood Books, Trowbridge

Contents

Acknowledgments

The fine photograph that we have used as a frontispiece appears by kind permission of Mrs. Gwen Robert. The top pictures on pages 69, 80, 94, 104, and 107, and the bottom ones on pages 102, 105, and 118 are from the Martin Collection at the Greenwich Local History Library. We are indebted to Julian Watson, the Librarian, for making copies available, and to Neil Rhind, the Martin trustee, for permission to publish them.

All readers of Neil Rhind's definitive histories of Blackheath will recognise how much our early captions owe to them. Mr Rhind has also very kindly read the Blackheath and Lee sections of the book, and made many valuable corrections.

We have received considerable help of various kinds from Godfrey Smith, an abundance of cinema lore, as always, from Ken George, and learned advice on points of detail from Frances Ward, Douglas Earle, and John King. Our thanks to all.

Introduction

We found it difficult to choose a title for this book. Our first thought was *Lewisham, Including the Part of Blackheath in the Borough of Greenwich, but Excluding Those Districts of the Borough of Lewisham known as Deptford, New Cross, the Northern Half of Brockley, Forest Hill, and Sydenham.* Our publisher, however, was inclined to think this a little lacking in the snap and pep which attract attention and sell copies. *Lewisham*, he said, might be more easily remembered. Luckily, what will not serve as a title may furnish out an introduction.

Included in the book are photographs of Blackheath, Lee, central Lewisham, Hither Green, Ladywell, Crofton Park, Catford, Bellingham, Southend Village, and Grove Park. Deptford, New Cross, and northern Brockley, which together make up the ancient and famous town of Deptford, are so rich in history that they deserve a new photographic study of their own, and will, we hope, one day receive it. They are therefore excluded. Sydenham and Forest Hill are omitted because a volume in this series has recently been devoted to them.

Our excuse for poaching in Greenwich is less solid. We might allege that Blackheath is one and indivisible, and that the photographic lens will always mock political boundaries. This will serve for our photographs of the Heath itself, but can scarcely justify our sallies into St John's Park and Blackheath Park. The truth is that the pictures were available, and we could not resist them.

One of the pleasures of compiling these books is the impulse they give to exploration. Duty has led us to many byways that would otherwise have remained only names, and the experience has tempered our accustomed gloom with some sparks of optimism. Lewisham has thrown away most of its older architectural treasures, but it was so richly endowed by the Victorians with examples of all their building styles that a hundred wars and half a dozen councils could not have destroyed them all.

In the backstreets, especially, many Victorian developments survive almost intact, and because they were designed for the middle classes, most of them are solid enough to house many more generations. Numerous hostile forces threaten their chances of doing so. The most serious danger is from the unchecked passion for alteration. Everywhere the fine detail of houses is obscured by pebbledashing, by unsuitable windows, by the destruction of gables and other roof features during re-tiling. Those who treat Georgian architecture in this way are widely condemned as vandals. We only regard Victorian buildings differently because they are still comparatively common, just as the work of the Georgians was when our grandfathers regarded it with contempt. It is certain, however, that future centuries will look upon the maltreatment of a 1760 or an 1860 house as equal acts of Philistinism. (Few 1960 houses, probably, will last long enough to become objects of veneration.)

For the moment, at least, Lewisham is predominantly a Victorian town. If it could only resolve seriously to defend and preserve this inheritance, those top-hatted builders of long ago might yet prove its unwitting saviours. Dozens of roads deserving the most careful protection could easily be cited, but we will content ourselves with a few illustrated in this book. Somerset Gardens is a fine, unspoilt example of Victorian design, and on a much larger scale Granville Park has survived with remarkably few alterations. Embleton Road, Westdown Road, Davenport Road, and George Lane only require a unified approach to decoration and a firmer control of unsightly alterations to regain much of their original style.

If they are allowed to survive, the large estates created by Cameron Corbett at Hither Green, and by the Forster family along the Bromley Road, in the last years of Victoria and during the reign of her son, are likely to be regarded with ever increasing favour. Both escaped from the Second World War with relatively light damage, but the greedy passion for extending houses when converting them into flats has since been much more destructive. Brownhill Road on the Corbett Estate is the saddest example of this.

We hope that our readers will find a tour of the streets illustrated here as interesting as we have done. The renewed speed of demolition in Lewisham gives warning, though, that this should not be delayed. Already a number of the buildings we found little altered may have been destroyed.

One
Blackheath

The east end of St.John the Evangelist seen from St. John's Park, c.1910. The church was built in 1852-53 (spire completed 1873), to the designs of Arthur Ashpitel.

St. Christopher's College trained girls as Sunday School teachers. It was founded at 22 and 23 Montpelier Row in 1908, but in 1917 moved to Westcombe House, now 27 Vanbrugh Park. This mansion had been built in 1883 for the soap magnate James Kolle Soames. It is seen in the centre of the view above, which dates from 1928, when the Mycenae Road wing (on the left) was added. The spire of St. John's can be seen between Westcombe House and the new building. The college chapel, seen below, and on the right in the top picture, was rebuilt in a very different style in 1965. With other alterations and extensions, the complex became the senior department of the Blackheath High School for Girls in 1994.

Ranger's House, on the Blackheath edge of Greenwich Park, was built in 1699 for Francis Hosier, a distinguished sailor, but is principally associated with the great Earl of Chesterfield, who in 1749-50 added the wing seen on the right of this picture of c.1900. In 1815 the house became the official residence of the Rangers of Greenwich Park, but it is now an English Heritage historic house museum.

Hyde Vale, this south end of which was formerly Conduit Vale, seen from the Heath in the early years of the century. The old ivy-covered house behind the tree had been the George and Dragon pub. It was demolished in the 1920s. The white building in the distance was Clifton House at the top of Crooms Hill, which was sadly pulled down in 1938.

Two Edwardian photographs of the bank holiday fun fair on Blackheath. The stalls were set up along the Shooters Hill Road, close to the Blackheath Gate of Greenwich Park. The top picture shows the view eastwards towards Vanbrugh Terrace and St. John's Church. On the left are the folly pond and a hard-pressed public convenience. The bottom picture features the corner of Chesterfield Walk, and the Heath Keeper's lodge (now, like the lavatories, boarded up) in the angle of Charlton Road and Shooters Hill Road.

The helter-skelter, and other terrifying attractions at the Blackheath fun fair, c.1905. At least, though, they provided good vantage points for photographers. Patrons who were lucky enough to survive the rides were just as likely to succumb to the local ice cream and other suspect fairground delicacies. This was the period during which the London County Council was trying to get these monstrous jamborees under control by severe restrictions on the number of stall-holders' licences.

The Whitefield pond was a popular paddling venue during the Blackheath fairs. The view here is northwards towards the Greenwich Park corner, and the more expensive bank holiday pleasures along the Shooters Hill Road.

The Blackheath Gate of Greenwich Park was the centre of the donkey hiring business at the fairs. This is one of the long established attractions, and formerly a most controversial one, because of the harsh treatment suffered by the animals over many decades.

The Heath in the 1920s, showing the trees around the Prince of Wales Pond on the right, and St. Germans Place beyond. In the distance can be seen the spire of St. James's Church, Kidbrooke (as it appeared before bomb damage, and rebuilding in a different style), and the familiar outline of Shooters Hill.

Blackheath Vale seen from Lloyd's Place, probably just before the First World War. The buildings in the centre of the picture were Talbot Houses, four large semi-detached properties of the late 1870s which were to be destroyed by a flying bomb in 1944. Goffer's House now occupies the site.

Two views of Morden College, the noble almshouses built by Sir John Morden between 1695 and 1700. On the left is the main entrance, looking the same in 1900 as it does today, except that the Victorian shutters have now been removed. In the pediment can be seen the statues of the founders, Sir John's placed there by Lady Morden in about 1720, and hers by her executors shortly after she died in 1721. The lower picture, taken from the garden in the 1920s, shows the chapel, and on the right the library.

The entrance to Morden College from the Heath early in the century. The college lodge is on the right, and above it can be seen Morden Villas, a pair of houses built in 1853-54, and destroyed by bombing in 1941. The modern 1 and 3 Morden Road have taken their place.

The former no.14, now no.18 Morden Road, seen from the garden shortly after 1900, perhaps while occupied by Major General Henry Crozier. The house, which was built in 1858-59, is little altered today.

Two early twentieth-century views of the Heath frontages of the Cator estate, which were built between 1793 and 1810. South Row, above, looks sadly different now because the fine houses in the centre of the picture were destroyed by bombing in 1940, and have been replaced by the over-praised Span boxes. Fortunately Colonnade House, on the right, has survived as a wonderful ornament to this corner of the Heath. Montpelier Row (below) has fared much better than South Row. The only house lost to bombing was no.17, the building most clearly seen in this picture, just left of centre. In 1959 it was replaced by a semi-detached pair, one part of which was originally occupied by James Callaghan.

St. Germans Place seen across the Prince of Wales pond, c.1912. This was ten years after the demolition of Kidbrooke Lodge, the large house which stood nearest to the Morden College entrance, but before there had been much development in Kidbrooke Gardens, the road formed through its site.

A busy cricketing scene in 1894. The part of the Heath between Blackheath Vale, Montpelier Row (shown here on the left) and All Saints' Church, was always crowded with squares, generally used by the junior and less fashionable clubs. The London County Council had only recently abandoned its first come, first served rule, and allowed teams to book their pitches in advance.

All Saints' Church and Royal Parade in the early 1920s, when no.7 Royal Parade, now 49 Montpelier Vale, was the Montpelier Motor Works. The church was built in 1857-58 (the spire in 1867), to the designs of Benjamin Ferrey. It had rather humble neighbours until 1861, when Royal Parade replaced the cottages that had previously stood on the Heath frontage of the village.

The view of All Saints' from Grote's Buildings, c.1914. On the right can be seen Eastnor House, a fine mid-eighteenth-century building which was then being used as the Dartmouth Home for Crippled Boys.

Holly Hedge House c.1914, when it was the headquarters of the 20th. Battalion of the County of London Regiment of the Territorials. The part of the house in the centre of this picture was built in about 1743-44. The doorway was part of a large early nineteenth-century extension, probably built for Edward Legge, Vicar of Lewisham and Bishop of Oxford. Holly Hedge House was badly damaged during the Second World War, and demolished in 1946.

Blackheath was once dotted with gravel and sand pits, most of which have been filled during this century. The old gravel pit at the top of Lewisham Hill is a rare survivor, but it was nearly lost to the Heath in the 1780s, when the original builder of the Hermitage tried to annex it as part of his garden. This photograph of about 1905 probably shows the eastern edge of the pit from near The Knoll.

Blackheath Hill viewed from the corner of Dartmouth Hill in about 1900. The houses on the left, formerly known as Collyer's Buildings, appeared at various dates between 1784 and 1805. All of them as far as no.98, the house with the white bay windows, still survive, although the stone-faced no.104 has been completely refronted.

Holy Trinity, Blackheath Hill and Shadwell House, no.79, in 1909. The church was built in 1839-40, wrecked by bombing in the Second World War, and demolished c.1954. The flats called Undercliff stand on its site at the corner of Maidenstone Hill. Shadwell House survived the Blitz, only to be swept away in 1968 for part of the development called Hollymount Close, though the site of the house itself has been used merely for a lawn. The winding path survives.

Part of Lansdowne Place, Blackheath Hill, c.1910, with the Green Man Hotel on the right. This was the most celebrated of the Blackheath inns. It was rebuilt in 1868-69, when the houses seen here replaced the original assembly rooms. All these properties were demolished in 1970-71, and have been replaced by the flats of Allison Close.

Dartmouth House in Dartmouth Row was probably rebuilt for the Second Earl of Dartmouth on his succession in 1750. It is seen here from Lewisham Hill shortly after it became the College of Greyladies (an Anglican religious community) in 1906. That was when the large wing was added.

Dartmouth Terrace in Lewisham Hill consisted of twenty houses. This 1914 photograph shows one of the two larger end properties, no.20 Dartmouth Terrace, later 39 Lewisham Hill, at the period when one Miss Blanchard was the occupant. Dartmouth Terrace was built in 1825, and largely destroyed by a flying bomb in June 1944. Burnett House is now on the site.

Development on Lewisham Hill began in the mid-seventeenth century with Colfe's School, but the oldest surviving buildings are houses of the 1860s. In this 1910 view from the bottom of the hill the taller houses are from that period, but the two on the far right, nos. 6 and 8, were built in 1890.

The new outpatients' department of St. John's Hospital in the 1920s. It was formerly the private house called Gotha Cottage, which stood at the corner of Morden Hill and Lewisham Road, some 150 yards south-west of the main hospital building. Gotha Cottage had been built in 1845, and was demolished with the rest of the hospital in the late 1980s.

Hanley Villa, no.25 Blackheath Rise, perhaps during the First World War. Blackheath Rise, a development of the early 1870s, was originally called Victoria Road. Hanley Villa, which was at first numbered 15, was built in 1877. It survives in good condition, but like most of the original Blackheath Rise houses, has lost much of its garden.

Granville Park is a highly moral road, presenting alternately either a delightfully easy primrose path from Blackheath to Lewisham, or a stern climb from Lewisham to Blackheath. It was perhaps this bracing emblematic character that encouraged the Kent Education Committee to establish a hostel there in 1907 for its young ladies attending Goldsmiths' College. Or possibly it was just that the houses were cheap at that moment. The Kent Hostel (now called the Granville Park Hall) occupies nos. 31 to 37, which were built in about 1866, rather later than some of the Granville Park houses. The road had been laid out in the 1850s. For other Goldsmiths' College hostels see pages 48 and 125.

Two
Blackheath Village and Park

Blackheath Village in the late 1930s, showing Sainsbury's shop at no.13, and at no.11 the leading photographic studio of the district, still trading as Wayland's, although Henry Wayland had died in 1922. It is now the Age Exchange Reminiscence Centre.

All Saints' Church and nos. 25 to 49 Montpelier Vale, c.1920. The nearer shops, running north from Tranquil Passage, were built in about 1882. The larger ones beyond (originally part of Royal Parade) date from the early 1860s.

All Saints' and Royal Parade, c.1905. Christy's Tea Rooms were at no.17 from 1904, and the Royal Victoria Cycle Co. had left no.16 by 1907. The drinking fountain (which survives intact) was the Blackheath traders' memorial of the Diamond Jubilee of Queen Victoria in 1897.

The Jubilee drinking fountain again, and the view down Tranquil Vale in the 1920s. The large block on the left, Highland House, was built about 1880, but the small terrace adjoining (nos. 58 to 68) is one of the oldest in the village. These cottages, which have been converted into shops since the 1830s, probably date from the last few years of the eighteenth century. Beyond them are nos. 54 and 56, and the Three Tuns public house, all rebuilt in 1884-85. The two spires above the Three Tuns roof belonged to the Wesleyan church in Blackheath Grove (destroyed by a V2 rocket in 1945) and to St. Michael and All Angels' in Blackheath Park. The smaller spire or turret on the right of the picture (directly above the head of the seated girl) belongs to St. Mary's Roman Catholic Church in Cresswell Park. Between the trunks of the trees on the right (which are still flourishing) can be seen a glimpse of the Crown, the oldest public house building in Lewisham.

Blackheath Village in 1905 or a little before. In the centre of the picture, between Bennett Park and Cresswell Park, stands the Alexandra Hall (built 1863), which survives today, much altered, as Lloyds Bank. The most prominent of the shops on the left was Stephen Jobbins's bakery and tea rooms at nos. 7 and 9. The cab ranks here and in Tranquil Vale were essentially for the use of Blackheath's City men arriving at the station.

Bennett Park, seen here c.1914, was a convenient but rather unfashionable Blackheath street, in which few families stayed longer than they had to. This is the south side, and shows houses built in the 1870s and '80s. The building at the end of the road, completed in 1886, was originally the Blackheath Art Club, but became famous in the 1930s and '40s as the headquarters of the G.P.O. Film Unit, a great pioneering force in documentary film making.

Blackheath Station and the centre of the village c.1930, with, on the right, Sainsbury's shop at the corner of Bennett Park, and the spire of the Wesleyan church in Blackheath Grove (see page 29). On the left is the spire of All Saints'. What is now Barclays Bank was built for the London and Provincial in 1888-89.

Blackheath Village from Lee Road, c.1914. On the left is the wall of the Blackheath Proprietary School, which had closed in 1907. At this time the classrooms housed, among other businesses, the Blackheath Press, which produced the *Blackheath Local Guide*.

Two views of the Lee Road entrance to Blackheath Village, in the late 1860s and c.1900. On the left of the earlier picture can be seen the Proprietary School lodge and the Railway Hotel or Tavern, and on the right the grassy bank removed when Beaconsfield Buildings replaced the old houses in the early 1880s. In the distance are the present 1 to 9 Blackheath Village before the shop-fronts were added. The 1900 view shows Beaconsfield Buildings. Nos. 8 and 9 were the nucleus of the business of Hinds and Co., which was soon to expand into the whole terrace, and to become Blackheath's own department store.

The Blackheath Concert Halls and Conservatoire of Music c.1900, four or five years after they were built. In the foreground is the garden of the Blackheath Park gate-keeper's lodge (see page 34), and on the left is part of Hinds's department store.

The Blackheath Congregational Church, in what is now Independents Road, was built in 1853-54. It was badly damaged by bombing in 1940, and reconstructed, with some of the original fabric retained, in 1957. A combination of rationalism and rationalisation led to the closure of the church in 1974, and it has now been converted into offices.

A characteristic scene of tranquil Edwardian prosperity in Blackheath Park. This road along the ridge was the height of Blackheathan gentility. The tradesmen on their rounds had only been admitted to this private domain after careful scrutiny by the Cator Estate gate-keeper. As usual, the majesty of the law was in close attendance in case of any dispute. The house on the left was the gate-keeper's lodge, built in the mid-1890s in replacement of one on the other side of the road. The new lodge was planned in conjunction with the Concert Halls by the same architects, Edmeston and Gabriel. Gradually the Cator Estate slackened its control over access to Blackheath Park, and the old lodge, now no.1, became an unconventional private dwelling.

The church of St. Michael and All Angels, Blackheath Park, with its delicate spire – the needle of Kent – in the late 1860s. It was built by the Cator family in 1830 as a proprietary chapel for the convenience of the tenants of their fast-growing estate. The design was by the prominent local architect, George Smith, who was also responsible for Blackheath Station.

The bridge over the Mid Kid Brook in what was, in 1905, part of Manor Way, but is now Brooklands Park. The photographer was standing south of the bridge, and looking towards Brooklands, George Smith's own house. It is not apparent from the picture that the stream widened into a boating lake beside the bridge. See also page 36.

The Manor Way

A similar view to the last, except that it was captured from the bridge. Brooklands Park retained this wonderfully rural appearance until the 1930s, when the ground to the left, mostly the garden of Brooklands, was opened up for development. The belt of trees on the right, and the land behind (the garden of Drake Court) were taken for the Brooklands Primary School and council housing in the 1950s. The parapet of the bridge seen on the left of the photograph on page 35 has been removed, and all trace of the river has been hidden on that side, but the right hand or eastern parapet does survive, and beyond it the boating lake has been retained as an ornamental feature of the housing estate.

Three
Lee

Lee Green and the entrance to Lee High Road c.1917, when the streets were full of Army Service Corps personnel from the Grove Park Hospital barracks. Many were billeted at Lee.

These houses on the north side of Lee Terrace, seen here during the First World War, were built in the 1830s by William Seager, a prominent figure in the development of Blackheath. The nearer six houses survive as nos. 47 to 61, but those in the distance were replaced by The Lawns in 1938.

The view up Lee Park towards Christ Church, c.1914. This was an old footpath, but building did not begin until the 1840s. The houses on the right of this picture, the old nos. 32 to 38, which dated from the 1850s and '60s, have been replaced by Shearman Road.

St. Margaret's, the parish church of Lee, has had a complex history. The first two known buildings stood on the north side of Lee Terrace. These two cards from about 1905 show the third and present church on the south side. It was built in 1839-41, architect John Brown of Norwich, but much of its modern appearance, especially of the interior, it owes to the remodelling carried out in the 1870s and '80s by James Brooks. The changes were financed by Frederick Law, the rector from 1873 to 1900. The lych gate, now removed to Church Terrace, was a memorial to his wife.

The garden front of The Cedars, Belmont Hill, while in use as a military hospital during the First World War. In the foreground are the mess tents. A patient has noted on the back of this photograph that "the Russians have their meals after we have ours".

Belmont Grove was carved out of the Cedars grounds in the late 1850s. Here, c.1900, it was looking quite extraordinarily idyllic, even though the great world (in the shape of Belmont Hill) was just beyond the distant gates. Despite the charm, this is a sad photograph for local historians, because the cameraman was standing outside Gothic House, and by swinging his lens a few degrees to the left could have captured a unique image of Ernest Dowson's birthplace.

The Lee Green end of Lee Road, c.1916. Except for the traffic the scene would not look much different today, if any photographer could be found reckless enough to attempt its duplication. The shop on the extreme right, no.141 Lee Road, was then occupied by Brozel Bros., watchmakers.

Lee Green from Lee High Road, c.1918. The local police had long been established here in a cottage, but the present station, seen on the right, was not built until 1904. The brightness of the brickwork on its shop-front extension suggests that the Prince Arthur pub, beyond the police station, had also been recently rebuilt. The garage at 1, Eltham Road was founded by Vivian van Damm in 1913.

A busy day at Lee Green, probably just after the First World War. The principal feature is the Old Tiger's Head, which was rebuilt in 1896. Between the buses entering and leaving Lee Road can just be seen the spire of Christ Church in Lee Park (see page 38).

Who would not infinitely prefer the comparative purity of these Victorian shops to the joyless modern scene? For this was the entrance to Burnt Ash Road from Lee Green, c.1920. The buildings on the left were swept away in 1967, to make way for the Leegate Centre. Sainsbury's supermarket now stands (or sprawls) on the right.

Cleveland House, 54 Eltham Road, which had been built in about 1863, was one of many large Lee properties requisitioned when the Army Service Corps came to Grove Park in 1914. This card was sent to his girlfriend by one of the soldiers billeted there. Cleveland House was demolished in 1959. Its site is occupied by the green at the corner of Eltham Road and Cambridge Drive, beside Leybridge Court.

Collingwood College in Leyland Road was a boarding school for girls run by the Palmer family from about 1870 (when this part of the road was built) until 1919. They had founded the school in the late 1860s at Collingwood Lodge, now 267 Lee High Road. This card was sent to a pupil by Miss Kate Palmer, with solicitous enquiries about a dolly. The school occupied six houses at its peak, but latterly was at nos. 46, 48 and 50 (seen here, with 50 on the left). They were demolished in 1962-63, and Carston Close now runs through the site.

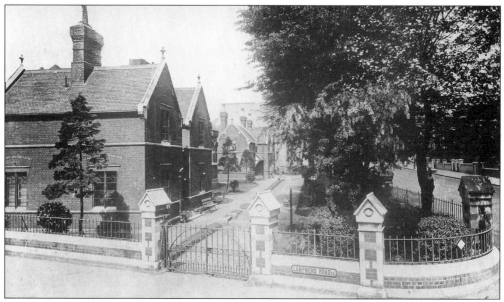

Boone's Almhouses were founded by Christopher Boone of Lee Place in 1683, but of the original buildings only the charming chapel remains, near the corner of Lee High Road and Brandram Road. The second almshouses and chapel (seen above in 1908) replaced them in 1875. They were themselves superceded in 1964 by the third and present almshouses in Belmont Park, but the buildings shown here do survive.

H.G. Walton's greengrocery business at 347 Lee High Road only survived from about 1905 to 1907. The shop stands next but one to the Old Tiger's Head, and the building reflected in the left hand window above was Dennis's butchers shop, at the corner of Burnt Ash Road. The photograph on page 37 makes this clear.

Lee High Road from the corner of Bankwell Road c.1918, showing the Woodman public house and the premises of A.Seymour, the draper, at 193 and 195. The shop on the right, the Lee Ironmongery Stores until 1912, had been untenanted for years, and may well have housed soldiers during the war. Both shops have now been replaced by a large garage.

The Lewisham end of Lee High Road in the early 1920s. The nearer shops on the right, part of Albion Terrace, are among the oldest in the road. They were built before 1814. All of these shops still survive, though some of them barely. No.68, then the premises of William Chandler the bootmaker, is now lying empty. It is hard to imagine the South Eastern Fur Stores flourishing here today.

Nos. 1 to 4 Manor Park Parade c.1906, just after Mrs. Janet Wood had established her toy and stationery shop at no.3. She also sold picture postcards, some of which can be seen (and coveted) in her window display. Eddowes's sweet shop was at no.4. Manor Park Parade had been built c.1895, on the garden of Lee Lodge.

An early view of Rembrandt Road, which with Murillo, Abernethy, and Lochaber Roads, was built in the 1890s over the garden of The Firs. This was a large house of about 1700 which stood in Old Road. At the bottom of the hill can be seen nos. 129 to 135 Lee High Road, which were pulled down immediately after the Second World War to make way for the telephone exchange, opened in 1947.

"Neath the shade of the dear old Elm Tree,
That so soon we shall never more see,
There stands our friend Kirk, all ready for work,
Neath the shade of the dear old Elm Tree."

The tree so feelingly commemorated in the lines on the back of this postcard was in the forecourt of Lee Baptist Chapel (built 1854, bombed 1941), at the corner of Eastdown Park. It was doomed because in 1906 Lee High Road was widened to accomodate tram lines. Kirk the cab horse had his stand here for years, as other photographs testify.

Pentland House, Old Road, which dates from about 1680, is one of the oldest buildings in Lewisham. When this photograph was taken in 1914 Goldsmiths' College had lately acquired it as a hostel (one of several featured in this volume, see pages 26 and 125) and the wing on the left had been added. A further gimcrack extension at the rear followed in the 1960s.

James Burke flaunting the fruits of his success as a builder outside his yard in Manor Lane, in about 1909. The headquarters of the firm was at 7 Rembrandt Terrace, later 210 Lee High Road, from 1896 until 1936. From 1910 it was known as Burke, Collins, and Co. The Manor Road building is now being enlarged and extensively altered.

Two animated views of the Manor House Gardens, above c.1905, and below in 1910. This park, formerly the private pleasure grounds of the Manor House, was officially opened in 1902, and the mansion became a library. The earlier picture shows the pond, for which see page 50, with the houses of Brightfield Road behind. Below is the Old Road entrance to the park. The flower bed occupies the site of the Manor House stables and coach houses, which were demolished in 1901.

A charming scene in Manor House Gardens in 1907, during those tranquil days of Edwardian high summer when a policeman was a universally honoured symbol of authority, and respect and reverence were the chief characteristics of children! The pond was not only an ornamental feature in the grounds of the Manor House. The earth excavated for its creation was used to cover the ice-house, and thus keep it cool, and the winter ice from the pond was stored there, ready to chill the lord of the manor's champagne during the summer.

The Northbrook School seen from Wantage Road, c.1906. It was founded as the Hedgley Street Infants' School in 1870-71. The boys' and girls' departments nearer to Taunton Road were added in 1884. The buildings were badly damaged in 1941, while the children were safe in Kent, and when the new school opened in 1957 it was for secondary pupils only. The original occupants, the infants, had been expelled.

Handen Road from the Burnt Ash Road end during the First World War. It was laid out in 1868, and the first houses were built a year or two later. The ones seen on the right here are nos. 6 to 12, built in about 1873, probably by George Gates.

The Church of the Good Shepherd, an unusual and attractive design of Ernest Newton, and greatly superior to his St. Swithun's at Hither Green, was built in 1881, but sadly destroyed by bombing in 1940. The present church, built in 1957, retains something of the same exterior appearance, but the interior (seen below in about 1910) is very different. The house beyond the church, no.31, is still standing.

The Burnt Ash Road Congregational Church was built in 1876, and destroyed by a flying bomb in 1944. Its replacement, now the United Reformed Church, appeared in 1955. The shops between the church and Lee Station, known as Upwood Terrace, date from about 1873.

The chief feature in this view of Burnt Ash Hill is the Crown Hotel at the corner of Corona Road. It was founded by one James Playford, as a beershop, in about 1870. The Crown survives little altered, except that the enlarged balcony no longer has a canopy, but many of the large houses that surrounded the pub in 1907 have been replaced by blocks of flats.

Newstead Road, which has been sadly truncated since the early 1970s by the council estate named after it, is seen here c.1905, during its prime. The road grew slowly from origins in the early 1870s. The view here is towards Burnt Ash Hill, with the surviving nos. 27 to 31 visible between the trees on the right.

The St. Mildred's Soldiers' Club was established during the First World War at the parish hall in Baring Road, where Gordon House now stands. The Army Service Corps soldier who sent this card in 1916 told his daughter that "this is the Hall where I write my letters to you and Mum".

Four
Lewisham North

The clock tower and what are now the Midland and Barclays banks, towards the end of the First World War.

Lewisham Road, c.1905. The photographer was standing not far from the Sydney Arms, and looking in the direction of Lewisham. The pillar box was (and still is) at the corner of Blackheath Rise. This was the smart residential part of the street, made delightful by the masses of mature trees in all the front gardens, but the houses have now gone, and many of the trees with them.

The working end of Lewisham Road at about the same time, with a fire engine galloping up from the station in Lindsell Street, Greenwich. The view is towards John Penn Street. On the right is the Ordnance Arms pub, which closed in 1909 – Doleman House is now on its site – and beyond it the railway bridge over the platforms of Blackheath Hill station on the Greenwich Park Branch.

A Rose Cottage laundry cart somewhere on its rounds. The date is about 1910, when William Annells was the owner. No.16 and the other houses in Drysdale Road were demolished in the mid-1960s, and their site is now occupied by Lethbridge Close.

Embleton Road was built by Samuel Jerrard of Loampit Vale in the 1890s. This photograph, taken from Vicar's Hill, shows no.135 (on the right) to no.117, probably in 1910. These houses are still standing in good condition, although the round-headed window in the wing of no.135 has been sacrificed for a single-storey extension towards the road. All the garden railings have gone, of course.

The Algernon Road Congregational Church (shown here c.1905) was built in 1884. James Cubitt, the architect, needed some ingenuity to squeeze it into a very narrow plot. The church was badly battered during the Second World War, and destroyed in 1944. The replacement church of 1953 has lately been demolished, and new housing is rising on the site.

Sandrock Road was one of several with faintly geological names that were built in the 1890s and during the early years of the twentieth century over the site of John Edmund Lee's Loampithill House and the Lee family's great brickworks behind. This is no.13 Sandrock Road, built c.1898. It is almost unchanged since this photograph was taken some eighty years ago.

The only substantial loss suffered by Beaufort Gardens since this photograph was taken before the First World War has been its name, for in 1939 it was re-christened Somerset Gardens. There has been some additional building at the neck of the road, and its quiet was somewhat disturbed by the building of a railway loop line in 1929, but it remains a pleasant Victorian backwater, with its green and its dignified houses of 1859-60. They were designed, as a speculation, by Alfred Cross, who also built the houses in Loampit Hill, on either side of Somerset Gardens. Some of these survive, including Beaufort Lodge, now the lurid no.62 Loampit Hill, which was Cross's own house.

The All Saints' Boys' Orphanage at the foot of Granville Park was built in 1885. In 1927 the premises were bought as an annexe to Colfe's School in Lewisham Hill, and painstakingly converted into laboratories, an art room, a library, and a swimming pool. All in vain, for the building was destroyed by a flying bomb in 1944. Part of the basement (the Colfe swimming pool) survived as the Granville Park Adult Education Centre and Youth Club. The photograph was taken in 1913.

St. Stephen's, seen here c.1905, is not one of Sir George Gilbert Scott's more memorable churches, though expensively furnished. It would no doubt look better if the intended tower had been built, but the soil on this riverbank was not firm enough to support it. On the left is the vicarage in Cressingham Road.

Although the Obelisk junction, seen here c.1920, retained this basic pattern so recently, it is already becoming hard to imagine. The only surviving element from this picture is Obelisk Buildings, on the left. The Duke of Cambridge and Shepherd's Place (to its left) were rebuilt in 1929 as Obelisk Parade, and these replacements, together with the old shops on the right, were swept away in 1992 to accommodate a huge new roundabout.

The High Street c.1920, showing the view north to the Duke of Cambridge. This postcard was published by Boots Cash Chemists, who had been established at nos. 76 and 78 (on the left of the picture) since 1908, and have remained ever since, although their shop has been rebuilt.

Ambitious Victorian drapers liked to give their shops names suggestive of sophistication, and containing a hint (usually mendacious) as to the source of the stock in trade. When the Chiesman Brothers acquired one of the central shops of Granville Terrace, or the High Pavement, in 1884, they called it the Paris House. The name evidently took the fancy of the local shoppers, for by the time this photograph was taken in 1918 they had bought out all their neighbours, and Chiesman's was the doyen of Lewisham's department stores. The firm were soon to rebuild the whole terrace in grandiose style, and expand hugely to the north. Could they have imagined that eighty years later their name would be fading from memory, and that even the buildings would be threatened with a similar fate? The view here is towards the Obelisk, with the Duke of Cambridge (see page 61) on the extreme left.

The Salisbury public house, above in 1915 and below c.1905, at both of which dates Charles Hutchinson was the landlord. The pub had been built in 1899 more or less on the site of the Lion and Lamb, one of Lewisham's oldest inns, but the replacement lasted only sixty years. The turning on the right between 82 and the pub, which then gave access to Tilling's stables, is now the northern entrance to the Lewisham Centre.

St. Mark's is one of the lost churches of Lewisham, and increasingly one of the forgotten ones. It was built in 1870 to serve the College Park estate. St. Mark's survived the war but not the peace, for in the 1960s it was declared redundant, and demolished in 1968-9. The site, at the corner of Clarendon Rise and Bonfield Road (that part of which was formerly St. Mark's Road) is now occupied by 41 to 53 Clarendon Rise and Summer House. The exterior of the church suffered, like St. Stephen's (see page 60), from the failure to complete the tower, but the interior view below shows that St. Mark's was not a trifling loss.

The clock tower and what is now Barclays Bank in 1912. "I hope you like the boy's face in the corner", wrote the sender of the card. Other points of interest are the spire of the Methodist Church in Albion Road (now Way), which was destroyed during the Second World War, and the little shops of the 1820s and '30s on the site now occupied by the post office.

Edginton and Son first appeared at 19 Lewis Grove, as pianoforte dealers, in 1913, and they were to remain until about 1930. The shops in Lewis Grove between Lee High Road and Mercia Grove (which included some old cottages from the days when this was the east side of the High Street) were all rebuilt, in a very ugly style, in the 1930s.

The clock tower c.1914, standing in its eccentric old position, so inconvenient to our master the motor car. The Duke of Cambridge can be seen in the distance on the left, and on the right is part of George Stroud's department store, which was taken over by the Royal Arsenal Co-Operative Society in 1926.

The centre of Lewisham c.1918, giving a good view of the 1840s shops at the corner of Avenue Road (on the left), which were among the first purpose-built ones in Lewisham. They were soon to be demolished as the chain stores moved in. On the right is the Albion, which was rebuilt after being destroyed by the High Street flying bomb, but then suffered a shameful decline into a building society branch.

Five
Lewisham South

Lewisham Market c.1918, before the campanile of the Roman Catholic church was built. To the left of the 'Garage' sign was the White Hart, a pub not rebuilt after bomb damage.

The Electric Palace was the second cinema in the old Borough of Lewisham. It opened in December 1909, some eight months after the Catford Electric Palace in Sangley Road. The architect, W.Hancock, adorned it with a frieze likely to be admired when the Parthenon is forgotten. In June 1914 the big attraction was "the world famous detective" William J.Burns in *The Exposure of the Land Swindlers*. The management was also wooing the Lewisham public with the slogan, "no need to travel: come and see the world from an armchair". There was such a gratifyingly warm response that the cinema was soon too small to satisfy the demand for seats, or armchairs, and in 1922 the Electric Palace was rebuilt on a much larger scale, and renamed the Prince of Wales. The new cinema had a distinguished career, until the arrival of sound clipped the wings of its celebrated orchestra. The Prince of Wales remained open until 1959, and was demolished in 1960. The Homestyle and Beatties shops are now on the site.

This pair of old cottages, clumsily Gothicised early in the nineteenth century, stood a few doors south of the White Hart (see page 67), the side of which can be seen on the right. When this photograph was taken in 1897 the cottages were awaiting demolition. Nos. 174 and 176 (Specsavers and The Gold Centre) are now on the site.

An eighteenth-century villa known as Elm House or Grove House stood at the corner of the High Street and Limes Grove until 1906, when it was replaced by the Prudential offices, which are seen here c.1914. Though now dwarfed, this was then (and for long afterwards) the biggest commercial building in the High Street.

St. Saviour's Roman Catholic Church as originally built in 1909. Before that the congregation had met at various houses and halls, including the school behind the church, which dated from 1898. The church was enlarged to its present impressive size in 1929, by the addition of the campanile and presbytery.

This Edwardian postcard of the Lewisham Congregational Church (built in 1866) is a valuable record, because the rich interior was gutted during the Blitz. The United Reformed Church now uses the building, which has been restored in a simplified form.

The Black Bull c.1904, about three years before it was rebuilt. It was known as the Black Bull or Bull for at least four hundred years, and has been the Fox and Firkin for about fifteen, so there is hope that it will one day revert. The adjoining shops, now nos. 300 to 314, which were built in the eighteenth century, and modernised late in the nineteenth, are among the oldest in the High Street.

The part of the High Street opposite St. Mary's Church kept its village atmosphere longer than any other, and even today retains a ghost of it. The most picturesque buildings were the seventeenth-century houses (long used as shops) seen on the right of this view from about 1918. They were smashed in the Second World War, and their site is now the forecourt of the Ladywell Leisure Centre. On the left is the fire station, for which see page 72.

Lewisham's third fire station, seen here c.1920, was opened in 1898, and replaced in 1967. The building has recently commenced a new career as a housing advice centre. Above the distant tram can be seen the rebuilt Black Bull (see page 71).

Another photograph from about 1920, and one which continues the story southwards. This time the main feature is the St. Mary's National Schools, on the right. In the foreground are the original classrooms of 1833. The white gable beyond belongs to the extension of 1860. There have been some practical modern additions to the rear of the school, but it still looks very much the same. Long may it remain!

A wonderfully detailed study of the High Street in 1910. The date can be fixed because the notice below the tree, just left of centre, reads 'SITE FOR UNITARIAN CHURCH'. This was built in the garden of Sion House (seen here in front of the tower of St. Mary's) in that year. It later became part of the old Lewisham Library, and was demolished in 1994 to make way for the new hospital extension. Sion House, formerly the George Inn, was built in 1732, ceased to be a pub some fifty years later, and was shamefully demolished in 1972. The library (for which see page 74) is to the left of the church tower. The building on the near side of it was Colfe's almshouses, built by the Leathersellers' Company in 1663-5 with funds left by Abraham Colfe, the vicar of Lewisham from 1610 to 1657. In 1905 the almshouses had been restored by the grateful citizens of the town. The next generation allowed them to fall to pieces after bomb damage.

What one must get used to calling the old Lewisham Library, seen a few years after it opened in 1900. A.R.Hennell's pleasing symmetrical design was disturbed in the late 1920s by a rambling extension at the rear, which it would be cruel to attribute to any architect. The building served Lewisham well until 1994, when it was replaced by the refurbished telephone exchange, which is bigger. The old library's future is now in the hands of a hospital trust, a prospect perhaps about as hopeful as the future of a mouse in the paws of a starving cat. There are several points of detailed interest in this photograph. Notice the early example of sponsorship by the *Daily Telegraph*, and also the group of precocious nicotine addicts on the left. The tall youth is smoking not one cigarette, but two. It cannot be the young Paul Henreid on holiday, as he was not born until 1907.

Two views of Lewisham Park c.1920, when it was still one of the smartest addresses in Lewisham. The open space was then a private pleasure ground for the benefit of the residents. Perhaps the most appreciative of the privilege were the pupils of the many private schools that had existed here since development began in the 1850s. The board on the left of the top picture (taken from outside the library) advertises one of them, the Lewisham Park School for Boys, which was a forcing ground for commercial clerks, Lewisham's staple product. It was at no.71. The lower picture shows the southern side of Lewisham Park, where most of the houses are still standing.

The Lewisham workhouse was built in 1817, and in 1836 became the headquarters of the Lewisham Poor Law Union, a combination of seven parishes. The original building is on the left of this Edwardian view. The matching wing in the centre was added in 1882-5. Both are now part of Lewisham Hospital and, externally at least, little altered.

Lewisham was crowded with wounded soldiers during the First World War, when many of its houses and institutions were turned into military hospitals. The Lewisham workhouse was one of the largest. These soldiers in their hospital uniforms were posed in the workhouse garden, with the western block of the infirmary behind them. The trees on the left were on the banks of the Ravensbourne.

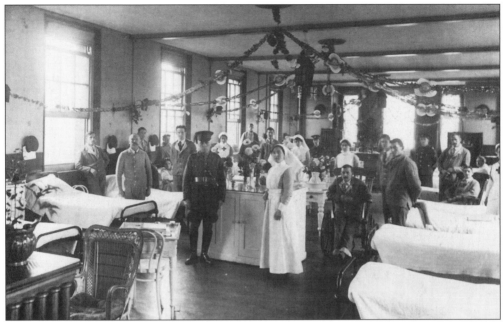

These two scenes inside Lewisham Military Hospital may show the same ward from different directions, but not necessarily, as they were built to a standard design. With windows wide open and masses of flowers scattered about, the celebration above cannot have been for Armistice Day or for Christmas. Perhaps it was Empire Day. There is only an even chance that the ward or wards shown here still survive, for many of the old workhouse and infirmary buildings were destroyed during the Second World War, when Lewisham Hospital had again been pressed into military service.

The irresistible growth of the workhouse and hospital has destroyed much of architectural and historical interest, and who would venture to say that the process is finished? The saddest losses were of Exchequer Place, a delightful terrace which stood next to the original workhouse, and the group of larger buildings to the north. This included Colfe's English School, and Dartmouth House, James Cole's private lunatic asylum. Some of these buildings were of great antiquity. The random disposition of the windows in the main house shown here betrays its considerable age. It was sometimes known as Woodham's, after William Thomas Woodham, the tenant in the 1840s and '50s. There seems a possibility that Woodham's served for a time as the offices of the Lewisham Board of Works, before the old town hall was built. The house was demolished c.1890 to make way for the workhouse infirmary. In the foreground of the picture is the bed of the High Street stream, which had run dry a year or two before this photograph was taken in the late 1850s.

Six
Hither Green

Arngask Road from St. Fillans Road c.1914, with no.1 on the left. These houses were built for Cameron Corbett by the firm of Bassett and Son in 1897-8.

The view from the railway bridge between Courthill Road and Morley Road in the 1870s, showing the Tonbridge Line, which opened in 1865. The Lewisham Congregational Church (see page 70) is on the left, at the bottom of Courthill Road.

An Edwardian view of the the rear of no.135 (formerly 75) Courthill Road. This and the neighbouring houses were built in the late 1870s. No.135 is still in good condition, though lacking the elegant garden furnishings. The mystery is how the photographer managed this shot without suspending himself above the railway cutting that runs at the bottom of the garden.

Hither Green Lane c.1912, showing St. Swithun's Church, which was built in 1892 to the designs of Ernest Newton (for whom see also page 52). The vicarage, on the right, was extended and altered at the same time, but is essentially still the early nineteenth-century house called the Chesnuts. It is, therefore, much the oldest building surviving in Hither Green.

This wintry photograph from about 1914 shows the view south towards the hospital from the shop-front roof of 174 Hither Green Lane, the premises of T.H.Fielding, the publisher of this card. The building on the left was the coach-house belonging to Clifton Cottage, a villa built in the early 1860s, which has been replaced by Mountsfield Court. Beyond it can be seen the surviving pair called Sidbury and Maple Villa (nos. 205 and 207), which were built in the late 1860s.

The Park Cinema at Hither Green seen from the hospital gates in late June 1931, about nine months after it was converted to show the talkies. The poster advertises a searing programme. For your immediate enjoyment Freddy Lonsdale's sophisticated wife-swapping comedy, *Canaries Sometimes Sing*, and for the second half of the week the 'It' girl, Clara Bow, vainly trying to extend her career into the sound era with *True to the Navy*. The Park, which was named after the hospital, had been opened in December 1913. It was one of the many cinemas designed by E.A.Stone of Norfolk and Prior, the Catford estate agents and surveyors, who specialised in that field. The Park closed in 1957, but the building still remains, shorn of its decorative features, as the L.D.C. windsurfing and sailing showrooms. The tree seen on the left edge of the top picture on page 86 stood just where the advertising board was in 1930.

The Springbank Road booking hall of Hither Green Station was the brainchild of Archibald Cameron Corbett, who lent the railway company the money to build it because he thought this access was essential to the prosperity of his St. Germans Estate. It fulfilled its original function magnificently, but later fell a victim to B.R. cuts. A timber yard now occupies the site, nearly opposite Duncrievie Road.

Brightside Road, which was built in the late 1890s, seen from Springbank Road, c.1906. No.5 is the house on the right. The shop at the corner of Nightingale Grove, in the distance, has now been converted into a house. The card was sent by the family at no.17, and they have marked their house with a cross.

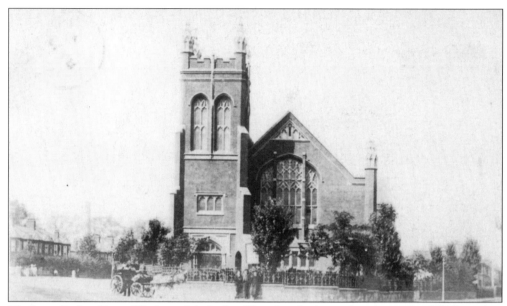

The huge Hither Green Wesleyan Methodist Church, which stood in the angle of Wellmeadow Road (right) and Hither Green Lane, was built in 1900, and destroyed by bombing in 1940. Its architects, Gordon, Lowther, and Gunton, grabbed and dominated this fine position. Littlebourne, the block of flats that has replaced the church, cowers in becoming shame at the back of the site.

The Methodist Church c.1905. On the left is the wall of no.328 Hither Green Lane (formerly 18 Ardgowan Gardens), a Corbett house built in 1898. The open space in the foreground was not covered by the present 330 to 340 until 1910. On the extreme right can be seen the premises of Jarman Bros., the builders, at no 385. Theirs was then the end house of the terrace.

The Mountsfield estate was purchased by the Lewisham and London County councils as a park in 1903, and Henry Tibbats Stainton's house was pulled down in 1905. These two postcards were issued not long afterwards. Both were taken near the site of the mansion. The view above is south-eastwards from the formal garden, with Stainton Road away to the left. In the bottom picture the view is eastwards towards the Stainton Road entrance, with the refreshment room (Stainton's museum) just visible on the left.

The Park Hospital, Hither Green, was built by the Metropolitan Asylums Board in 1896, and is being demolished by the Lewisham N.H.S. Trust a century later. It was originally a fever hospital for London as a whole. The architect was Edwin T.Hall, who here began a distinguished career as a designer of hospitals. This view across George Lane was taken from the roof of Beacon Lodge, the house demolished to make way for the Park Cinema and the adjoining shops.

The porter's lodge of the Park Hospital before the First World War. This is the building seen, from the other side, in the centre of the top picture. The decorative doorway has now been replaced by something much less interesting, and a large porch has been added. The main gates are just out of picture on the right.

Two more views of the Park Hospital, c.1913. The one above shows, on the left, the wing of the maids' home (now St. John's House) which was destroyed in the Blitz. Beyond it is Birch House, and in the distance the administration building opposite the main gates. The picture below shows the recently demolished nurses' home, with a giggle of nurses on the balcony. On the far side of the distant wing lies Stainton Road. Nurse Davies, who sent this card, reported that "I am sleeping in the room with the cross".

Nos. 185 (on the left) to 207 George Lane, c.1914. These houses at the eastern end of the road, opposite Hither Green (the Park) Hospital, look no different today. They were built in 1909-10.

These houses, built c.1897, were among the first on the Corbett Estate. They are nos. 294 to 302 Hither Green Lane, between Ardgowan Road and Minard Road. In their early years they were known as 1 to 5 Ardgowan Gardens. No.294 was the surgery of Doctor Cunningham Park when this photograph was taken, probably in 1907.

Two scenes on the Corbett Estate from postcards sent in 1905. Broadfield Road, seen above from the Brownhill Road end, was built c.1900. The nearest house is no.1. The southern boundary of the estate is formed by Hazlebank Road, which is shown below from the corner of Minard Road, with the wall of Hither Green Cemetery in the distance. Hazelbank Road was built by James Watt (see pages 115 and 116) in 1901-2. Neither road is greatly altered.

The parish church of the Corbett Estate was inevitably dedicated to the patron saint of Scotland. Saint Andrew's was built in 1904 to the designs of P.A.Robson, and is shown here when spanking new. The house on the right is no.180 Sandhurst Road, which was looking quite weathered in comparison with the church, though itself not more than five years old.

Torridon Road from Brownhill Road, c.1919. The church hall was built for the Bible Christians in 1900 (architect, E.J.Hamilton), at the same time as these houses, but by the time the church itself (on the near side of the hall) was added in 1913, amalgamations had transformed it into the United Methodist Church. Hall and church are about to be demolished.

Seven
Ladywell and Crofton Park

One of the rustic bridges over the Ravensbourne in the Ladywell Recreation Ground (now Ladywell Fields) seen c.1900, with the houses of Malyons Road in the distance, across the railway line.

The St. Mary's parish hall and the Ladywell public baths seen from the bridge c.1905. The hall was built in 1891. Its architect was Albert L.Guy, the man responsible for Prendergast's School (page 104) and the Tiger's Head, Southend (page 119). The baths, designed by the Dickensian sounding firm of Wilson, Son, and Aldwinckle, were built in 1884. They were replaced by the High Street swimming pool in 1965, but the building survives, minus the cap of the tower.

St. Mary's Church seen in and across the Ravensbourne from Ladywell Recreation Ground, c.1918. The lady so deeply absorbed in her magazine was sitting in the new section of the St. Mary's graveyard, which was added in two stages, in 1791 and 1850, in a vain attempt to keep up with the growing population and mortality of Lewisham.

The bridge leading from Ladywell Recreation Ground into the footpath from Ladywell Road to the High Street, as it appeared c.1918. The St. Mary's graveyard (see the opposite page) is on the right. Even today this area, so close to the centre of the town, retains a pleasant hint of the rural.

The water meadows along the Ravensbourne valley between Ladywell and Catford were acquired by the Lewisham and London County councils in 1889, and converted into the attractive park which they called, unromantically enough, Ladywell Recreation Ground. It is characteristic of our age to have made the park less attractive while prettifying its name.

Ladywell Bridge, which was built in 1830 to replace a wooden footbridge and ford, pictured in the late 1850s, when the house on the right (now 53 Ladywell Road) was just completed. In the distance can be seen the glebe land of the parish, which provided part of the vicar's income. The hedgerow cutting across the glebe marks roughly the line later taken by Vicar's Hill, as seen below.

Vicar's Hill from the corner of Algernon Road c.1914, with the turning to Algiers Road on the left. Samuel Jerrard built the nearer houses in the late 1880s, and had nearly completed Vicar's Hill by 1914. Compare this with the view opposite.

Ladywell Village sprang into existence during the 1780s when a number of cottages, mostly wooden, were built on the wasteland beside the road. The main group was on the north side, between the modern Algernon Road and Adelaide Avenue. When these cottages were pulled down in the 1890s they left a large plot for redevelopment, and this was gradually filled by Gillian Street and the major terrace of shops known as The Pavement, part of which is seen here c.1908. These shops, the first to be built, were nos. 4 to 1 The Parade, now 224 to 218 Algernon Road. No.1 was James Haydon's dairy, which is seen more clearly in the frontispiece to this volume. The shops are still intact, if a little battered. In the background is the junction of Algernon Road and Vicar's Hill. The house on the right, 214 Algernon Road, was long a doctor's surgery. It was demolished in about 1968, and has been replaced by a small block of flats.

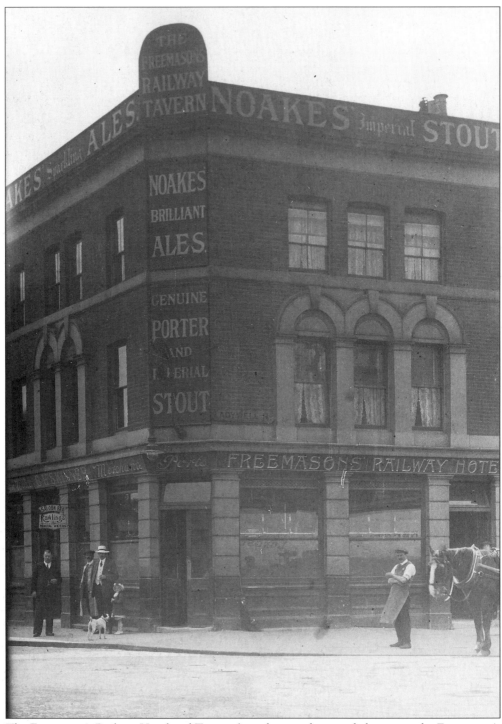

The Freemason's Railway Hotel and Tavern (now less cumbersomely known as the Freemason's Arms) has stood at the corner of Ladywell Road and Railway Terrace since the mid-1860s. This photograph was taken when George Henry Skinner was the landlord, between 1911 and 1919. He is probably the man on the left.

Montague Avenue seen from Tressillian Road in 1910, when this was Deptford gazing across the boundary at Lewisham. These houses, nos. 15 to 28, were built in the years around 1900. The Hilly Fields open space was still looking rather new and raw in 1910.

The eastern end of Ladywell Road c.1910, with the tower of St. Mary's in the distance. The houses on the left, nos. 129 to 143, were built in the late 1880s, the ones on the right, at the far corner of Francemary Road, c.1900. The trees were in the gardens of Adelaide Avenue.

The Hilly Fields open space, which was officially opened to the public in 1896, was a favourite with the panoramic photographers. The top picture, taken c.1920, shows the view eastwards over Lewisham from the path that runs down from the old Brockley County School towards Vicar's Hill. On the left is the back of Fairview, a house long demolished. It stood in Cliffview Road. The picture below dates from about 1910. The roofs in the foreground were in Algiers Road (long before Veda Road was built), and beyond can be seen Ladywell, with the Freemason's Arms in the centre (see page 96), and St. Mary's on the left.

The West Kent Grammar School on Hilly Fields was founded by John Bell, formerly headmaster of the Greenwich Proprietory School. The architect, W.Charles Evans, produced a grandiose design, but only the central block, seen here from Adelaide Avenue, was built, in 1884-5. This was because of the financial problems that dogged the enterprise, and led to several changes of ownership before the school closed in 1905. It was bought by the London County Council and reopened as the Brockley County School. This view of the building is unfamiliar because the L.C.C. twice extended it on this side, in 1913-14, and in 1921, hiding the original fabric. Evans's design can still be examined from the northern side of the building. Brockley County School closed its highly successful career in 1983, and since then the building has passed unhappily through various hands, and become increasingly bedraggled. It is now about to start a more hopeful chapter in its chequered history as the new home of Prendergast's School (see page 104). Councils used to let the grazing rights of their parks to local farmers. The sheep provided revenue and also cut down the mowing bills considerably.

Hilly Fields, the West Kent Grammar School, and Eastern Road, c.1904. Eastern Road is notable as the home of Henry Williamson, whose novels give such a vivid picture of the town. Except for the war years, when he was on active service, he lived at no.11 (now 21) from 1900, when the house was new, until 1921. As he was born in 1895 Williamson could be one of the boys in the photograph.

The chief interest of this view of Brockley Road is provided by the buildings on the right, between Ivy Lane and Adelaide Avenue, which were bombed in April 1941, and have been replaced by flats. The two end shops were built in the 1890s for monumental masons – this being by the cemetery gate – but the rest of the terrace dated from 1901. Chappell's shop, on the left, was built c.1897.

The Ladywell and Brockley cemeteries were opened in 1858, in response to public anxiety about unhealthy overcrowding in suburban churchyards. Although both were in Lewisham, they were originally called Lewisham and Deptford cemeteries because they belonged to the parishes of St. Mary and St. Paul. These postcards date from about 1905. The one above shows the view from the Ladywell cemetery lodge, and below are the Church of England and Nonconformist chapels in Brockley cemetery. They were destroyed in the Second World War, and have been replaced by a single building.

No volume of Lewisham photographs would be complete without a picture of the Brockley Jack, which is seen here c.1895, when the landlord was James Law. This was three years before the lamentable rebuilding of this ancient landmark.

College Farm stood next to the Brockley Jack (which is just out of picture on the right), divided from it only by the ancient track now known as the Brockley Footpath. The farm had just ceased working when this photograph was taken (from Brockley Road) in 1897, for its fields had been eaten by railway lines and new streets. The last farmer was Arthur Rudyard, who gave up in 1895. The farmhouse survived until about 1913.

Eight
Catford

Lewisham Town Hall and the tram shelter c.1930. The gates of the council yard can be seen on the right, where the concert hall was to be built a few years afterwards.

The chief interest of this 1870s view north from the gates of Rosenthal is the "elaborate building of imposing elevation" on the left. It was the stable of a villa called Meadowcroft, which stood on what is now the line of Bradgate Road. The architectural flourish was not for the benefit of the horses, but of the billiards players upstairs. The stable survived the demolition of the house, and most of it remains incorporated into the shop next to Prendergast's School.

The Lewisham Grammar School for Girls, better known as Prendergast's, seen from the corner of Hawstead Road and Blagdon Road in about 1905. At first glance the building may not appear much altered, but in fact it was extended to the right in 1907, and raised a storey in the late 1920s, after which the turret was neatly replaced. Despite these and other enlargements the school is still too small, and Prendergast's is about to take flight for Hilly Fields (see page 99).

The George Inn and the entrance to George Lane c.1918, when the Catford Bon Marché, originally a drapery, had become one of Knapton and Sons' ironmongery shops. Joseph Gatcombe's Dairy was at no.1 George Lane until 1919. The George probably lost its stable block (the white building in the centre) as a result of bomb damage in 1940. The horse trough only disappeared quite recently.

An excellent view of Navy Place in 1897. The two large brick houses, nos. 7 and 9 Rushey Green, were built in 1744, and the wooden cottages on either side c.1770. The side of the George can just be seen on the extreme left. Navy Place was destroyed by bombing in October 1940, and has been replaced by the Lewisham Social Security Office.

The houses on the south side of George Lane, behind the pub, were built c.1815, but development in the rest of the road did not begin until the second half of the century. This view from about 1904 shows the gabled houses numbered 51 to 69, which were built in the late 1870s. On the right is the entrance to the Doctor's Field, three acres belonging to the Bridge House Estate. They were not built upon until 1905.

Davenport Road was formed in the early 1890s over the grounds of Rosenthal. This photograph of about 1906 shows the present 9, 11, etc. (built by 1893), and on the left no.3, which was added a few years later. These houses look much the same today. The absence of any nos. 5 and 7 is explained by no.9 having been built first. Four houses were expected to be fitted into the gap, but only nos. 1 and 3 appeared.

A very unfamiliar Rushey Green in 1897. No.54 still survives at the corner of Patrol Place, and the shops on the far left are the present 74 to 78, beyond Bradgate Road. To the right of the lamp post is the Plough and Harrow. The wooden cottages were replaced, c.1900, by the large Sainsbury's shop (now a pawnbroker's) and its neighbour, and the Job Centre stands today on the site of the Hatch and Hatch offices.

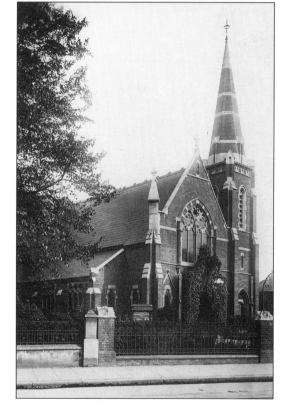

The Catford Wesleyan Church in Rushey Green, c.1914. It was built in 1896, on part of the site of Rosenthal, and demolished in 1966-67. The large shop in front of Capital House now occupies its site.

The Lewisham Hippodrome music hall, at the corner of Brownhill Road, and the Queen's Hall cinema next door, c.1919, shortly before the Whitehall Memorial was moved here from Catford Road. The Hippodrome had opened in 1911, the Queen's Hall in 1913. Both were demolished in 1960, and have been replaced by Eros House.

Rushey Green in the early 1920s, showing the booking hall of the Hippodrome on the right, and the Whitehall Memorial Fountain on the left. It had been built outside the Town Hall in 1898, with funds left by Michael Whitehall, was moved here in 1920, and vanished from the ken of history in the 1950s.

No.79 Glenfarg Road, probably c.1914, when it was occupied by the Russell family. It was built in 1899, and survives, though blighted by pebbledashing and unsuitable windows. This was the smallest type of house built by Cameron Corbett on his St. Germans Estate. Its cheapness, and the attractive incentives offered with it, helped to change the social complexion of Lewisham during the Edwardian era.

The point at which Sandhurst Road becomes Sangley Road has scarcely changed since this photograph was taken c.1918. On the right is the back of 61 St. Fillans Road. The lady who sent this postcard home to a village near Middlesbrough in 1924 represented herself as "about scared to death there is that much traffic".

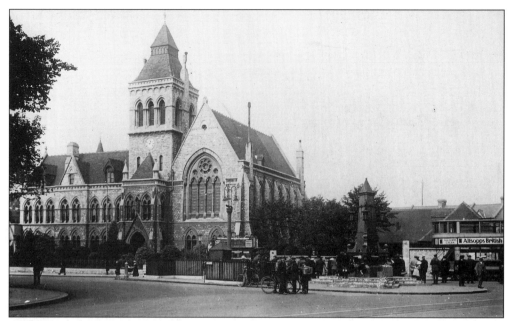

Lewisham Town Hall c.1918, above, and in the mid-1930s. In the earlier view the Whitehall Memorial still features (see page 108), but by 1935 it had long been replaced by the tram shelter. The photograph below also shows the concert hall extension, which was opened in 1932, and on the left St. Laurence's Church, which was demolished in 1968. Laurence House took its place after a delay of only twenty-two years.

The tranquility of this Edwardian scene is rather misleading, as the booking hall of Catford Bridge Station is visible between the trees on the right (across the Ravensbourne), and the platforms of Catford Station are just out of sight on the left. What is more, the trees on the left were growing above the mighty Bell Green Sewer.

Catford Bridge in about 1914, shortly after it was widened. This was suggested in 1903, but disputes between the L.C.C. and Lewisham Council delayed work until 1911-12, when a planned tramway extension suddenly made it urgent. On the right is the old town hall, and on the left the terrace of shops called Station Buildings, which had been reconstructed because of road widening for the bridge.

Catford Station, on the South Eastern and Chatham Railway, was opened on the 1st of July 1892. This was the original booking hall in Ravensbourne Park. It was closed and demolished some years ago, and access to the platforms is now from the 'down' side.

When Ravensbourne Park was laid out in the 1820s several meadows were set aside to preserve the open character of the estate, but as the century proceeded most of them were surrendered to the developer. Westdown Road was formed early in the 1870s, and largely completed by 1880. Most of its original houses survive, including Fern Lea, no.15, the one seen here. It has swopped some of its Victorian detail for a satellite dish and a burglar alarm.

St. Dunstan's College in the 1930s, looking very much as it did when opened in 1888. There have since been additions to the school, but this original block is not changed. The view could scarcely be reproduced, though, as it is always obscured by traffic and exhaust fumes. The bushes have naturally been sacrificed to the interests of the motorist.

St. Dunstan's seen from the corner of Beechfield Road in 1909. The late 1870s houses on the right are still standing, but the ones on the left have been demolished. They were nos. 371 and 373 Stanstead Road, which had been built c.1870.

The Catford Hill area was sparsely populated until the early decades of the nineteenth century, when a few villas were built for the growing numbers of City men moving to the district. The Chestnuts (later no.45 Catford Hill) was one of a pair built c.1815. It was gradually surrounded with loud Victorian neighbours, but survived until destroyed during the Second World War. Its site is now the entrance to the park.

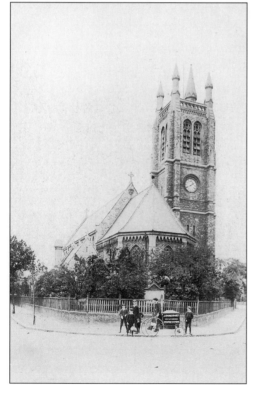

St. George's Church, Perry Hill (really in the fork of Woolstone and Vancouver Roads), seen here on an Edwardian afternoon when it was young, and strong, and beautiful, is now sadly old and decayed. It was built in the late 1870s, and seems likely to fall down tomorrow. The playful delivery boy outside was from the Sainsbury shop at 30A Catford Hill.

The Forster family owned more land in Lewisham even than the Earls of Dartmouth. Their Sangley Farm estate, on the eastern side of Bromley Road, was developed for them between 1902 and the 1920s by (among others) the eminent Scottish builder James Watt, who was also responsible for the cinemas at the junction of Bromley Road and Sangley Road. Here are Culverley Road (above), seen from Inchmery Road c.1909, and Inchmery Road from Thornsbeach Road (with no.113 on the right) c.1914. Watt built these houses, which are as trim and prosperous now as then, in and around 1905.

Bromley Road in 1930, showing the view south towards the junction with Canadian Avenue, where a Corrall and Co. coal delivery cart can be seen plodding towards the centre of Catford. The houses on the right and in the centre, most of which are still standing, were built in the 1890s by James Watt and others. The house on the left, partly masked by trees, was Sangley Farm, over the fields of which Watt had recently led the way in the building of ten streets (see page 115). After a spell as the Forster estate office the old farm became a school (the Sangley House School) in 1905. It is still surviving, as the Priory House School, which must make it one of the oldest centres of private education in Lewisham. This is a delightfully refreshing oasis of antiquity in an otherwise entirely modern stretch of suburbia.

Nine
Southend and Grove Park

The view along Southend Lane towards the village in 1916. The card was sent home by a soldier to assure his friends that "Catford is quite like the country in some parts".

Bromley Road during the First World War, clogged, as it usually was, with the vehicles of the Army Service Corps. On the right are the Bromley Road bus garage, which had opened in 1914, and the houses called Zetlands and Aubrey, which were destroyed in 1940. An extension to the garage was built on their site. The tent is pitched in the field where Hatcliffe's Almshouses and Bromley Road Library were later, successively, built.

When this photograph of Bromley Road was taken in 1897 Ivy Cottages were the premises of Thomas and Elizabeth Cooper's laundry, which used the Ravensbourne water running at the bottom of the garden. On the right were Bellingham Cottages, and on the left the site of the King's Arms pub, which was demolished in 1858. Ivy Cottages survived until about 1954, when they were replaced by the flats called Dunster House.

Bromley Road in the 1920s. A.J.Allen established his garage at the corner of Whitefoot Lane in 1923. On the far corner was Southend Hall, the old Forster home, which was hugely extended while it was a film studio from 1914 until 1923. The Tiger's Head is on the right. The shop beyond Southend Lane had a brief existence: it was built on part of the site of the lower mill in about 1924, and badly damaged in the war.

The Tiger's Head at Southend was rebuilt to the designs of A.L.Guy in 1901-2, some ten years before this photograph was taken. This was the period in which Lord Forster abandoned Southend Hall, which stood behind the tree on the right. On the left is the entrance to Southend Lane, then still very narrow. The Tiger's Head was destroyed by a flying bomb in 1944, and not rebuilt until 1958.

Park House, sometimes called Southend Park, was the manor house of Bellingham, and one of the chief mansions of the parish of Lewisham. It stood in Bromley Road, on the site now occupied by the flats called Falkland House, or perhaps rather the lawn in front of them. The old house was the home of Mrs. Inwin, the mother of Lady Falkland, and also of Thomas Hicks, a leading figure in local affairs between 1760 and 1780. In the 1790s Park House was rebuilt by Robert Saunders (1754-1825), a surgeon who had made a fortune in the service of the East India Company. He had obtained a lease for three lives, and the Saunders family continued to live here occasionally until the 1850s. When this photograph was taken, c.1920, the house was being run as a residential hotel by Thomas Guntrip, a local bookmaker. The Park was wrecked by a flying bomb in 1944, and demolished the next year. Flower House was also ruined during the war, which thus brought an abrupt end to Southend's great days.

Southend Village seen from Beckenham Lane, now Beckenham Hill Road, in the late 1890s, when George Hollingbery was landlord of the Green Man. This was the second pub, which replaced the original cottage c.1860. Vine Cottages, to its left, which were replacements for some ancient houses pulled down about 1870, lasted only until the Second World War.

A similar scene from a different angle, and a few years later, when trams were threatening momentous changes in the village. The building on the right in both pictures was the village bakery and post office. It was demolished in the 1920s when the Green Man was rebuilt on a much larger scale.

The three side turnings from Southend Village were famous for their beauty. Beckenham Lane, below, retains just a hint of its old charm, but Southend Lane (page 117) and Whitefoot Lane, seen here c.1910, have been utterley ruined. This is the view up the hill, with the fence of Lord Forster's Southend Hall garden on the right.

Beckenham Lane, now Beckenham Hill Road, c.1914, with the Green Man in the distance. The trees on the right were in the garden of Flower House (see page 120), the largest mansion in the village. It was then Dr. Charles Bullmore's private lunatic asylum. The Great War was about to give it a great influx of patients.

The Upper Mill at Southend Village late in the nineteenth century, after it had been considerably enlarged by Jacob Perry. As corn milling came to be increasingly monopolised by the big steam mills the Perry family moved into farming, and eventually into the timber business. Their house and part of the mill survived until the 1960s, when Caroline Court was built on the site. The mill pond, seen here, was used by the Perrys as watercress beds. Chelford and Bamford Roads have now taken its place.

Like any new town, Grove Park (which was created in the 1870s) had to have its shopping centre. It consisted, modestly enough, of The Terrace in Baring Road, seen on the left above, which was built in the late 1870s. The photograph below features part of the Terrace (now rebuilt after bomb damage) and shows its convenient relationship to the Baring Hall Hotel, the premier pub of the district. It was founded by John Pound, the father of the suburb, in the early 1880s. On the right is the station, the opening of which in 1871 had called Grove Park into existence.

Eversfield, no.251 Baring Road, was built c.1880, and in 1907 became a Goldsmiths' College hostel under the new name of St. Michael's. It was for thirty Church of England women. The house was demolished c.1950, and the Sandstone Estate now covers its site. For other Goldsmiths' hostels see pages 26 and 48.

When the Army Service Corps took over the Greenwich Union Workhouse at Grove Park in September 1914 the local community hurried to provide for the social needs of the soldiers. Several clubs were established, including the one at St. Mildred's church hall (see page 54). The most prominent was the Grove Park Soldiers' Institute at Maresfield, Baring Road, seen on the right here early in the war. The house has been rebuilt as nos. 337 and 339, but the plane trees remain.

Grove Park Hospital from the air.

This aerial view taken in the 1920s, when Grove Park Hospital was still surrounded by fields, suggests what a shock this huge complex must have been to Grove Park when it was built as a workhouse by the Greenwich poor law authorities between 1900 and 1902. That Thomas Dinwiddy's design was a prize winning one can have been of little comfort to the owners of the big houses in The Avenue (now Somertrees Avenue) in the bottom left of the picture, who had been used to looking out over farmland. The houses in the bottom right were built after the workhouse, the taller ones in Marvels Lane (called Marvels Terrace) in 1905-7, most of those in Fairfield Road in the early 1920s. On the far side of Marvels Lane, to the right of the hospital, are Sydenham Cottages, the oldest surviving houses in Grove Park, although they were only built in the 1860s. Grove Park Hospital was closed in 1994, and all but the lodges and administrative blocks have now been demolished. The new housing on the site is not likely to enrage the district as the workhouse did. It may not even be noticed, as it is all in the bland, inoffensive 'Nineties mode. Beyond it, in Mottingham, some agricultural land still survives.

During its five years as the No.1 Reserve Mechanical Transport Depot the old workhouse at Grove Park was a temporary (often an extremely temporary) home for many thousands of soldiers on their way overseas. In addition to those crammed into the workhouse itself there were large numbers in huts and tents in the fields for miles around (see page 118). This was excellent news for the postcard publishers. Here are two of the very many cards they produced for sale to the soldiers.

Baring Road south of Grove Park remained rural until the 1920s. This photograph looks north from the bridge where Baring Road becomes Burnt Ash Lane. The bridge crossed the small stream, a tributary of the Quaggy, which marked the boundary of Lewisham and Bromley. Today the stream has been buried like a guilty secret, Launcelot Road has been built across the field on the left, and all is dullest suburbia.

The junction of Marvels Lane and Riddons Road, c.1930. This was the entrance to the Grove Park Estate, which was built by Lewisham Council on 44 acres of Lord Northbrook's farmland between 1926 and 1929. The houses in the centre, part of the estate, are nos. 1 to 7 Riddons Road. The older properties on the left, Montraive and The Briars in Grove Park Road, have been replaced by a youth club.